The Unexplained

ALIEN VISITS

Extraterrestrials, UFOs, and Otherworldly Encounters

by Spencer Brinker and Stuart Webb

Minneapolis, Minnesota

Credits
Cover and title page, © Vegorus/Adobe Stock; 4–5, © danielegay/Adobe Stock; 6–7, © Maxim Khytra/ Adobe Stock and © Jana/Adobe Stock; 6TR, © Public Domain/Wikimedia; 6BR, © LMPark Photos/ Shutterstock; 8TL, © Chronicle/Alamy; 8BR, © Mary Evans Picture Library; 8–9, © jakartatravel/Adobe Stock and © aleciccotelli/Adobe Stock; 10TL, © Public Domain/Wikimedia; 10B, © Bettmann Archive/ Getty Images; 11TR, © Public Domain/Wikimedia; 12, © Amir Bajric/Adobe Stock; 13, © Sam Pollitt/Alamy and © stocker/Adobe Stock; 14TR, © Public Domain/Wikimedia; 14BL, © Public Domain/Wikimedia; 15BL, © Chronicle/Alamy; 16–17, © Dave Jonasen/Shutterstock and © sss78/Adobe Stock; 17BR, © Johnson Space Center/NASA; 18–19, © JJW Photography/Adobe Stock; 20–21, © stanislav_mukhin@/Adobe Stock; 22TR, © Chronicle/Alamy; 22BL, © Mary Evans Picture Library; 22BR, © Mary Evans Picture Library; 23, © Chronicle/Alamy; 24–25, © Public Domain/Wikimedia; 27, © Gamma–Rapho/Getty Images; 29, © Universal History Archive/Getty Images; 30–31, © jackienix/Adobe Stock; 32, © Mykola/Adobe Stock; 33MR, © Bettmann Archive/Getty Images; 33BR, © Carmen K. Sisson/Cloudybright/Alamy; 37BL, © Ajotte Collection/Alamy; 38TR, © Fairfax Media Archives/Getty Images; 38B, © Jim Dyson/Getty Images; 43BL, © Public Domain/Wikimedia

Photo Illustrations by Kim Jones.

Bearport Publishing Company Product Development Team
Publisher: Jen Jenson; Director of Product Development: Spencer Brinker; Managing Editor: Allison Juda; Associate Editor: Naomi Reich; Associate Editor: Tiana Tran; Art Director: Colin O'Dea; Designer: Kim Jones; Designer: Kayla Eggert; Product Development Specialist: Owen Hamlin

Statement on Usage of Generative Artificial Intelligence
Bearport Publishing remains committed to publishing high-quality nonfiction books. Therefore, we restrict the use of generative AI to ensure accuracy of all text and visual components pertaining to a book's subject. See BearportPublishing.com for details.

Library of Congress Cataloging-in-Publication Data

Names: Webb, Stuart, author. | Brinker, Spencer, author.
Title: Alien visits : extraterrestrials, UFOs, and otherworldly encounters / by Stuart Webb & Spencer Brinker.
Description: Minneapolis, Minnesota : Bearport Publishing Company, [2025] | Series: The unexplained | Includes bibliographical references and index.
Identifiers: LCCN 2024034992 (print) | LCCN 2024034993 (ebook) | ISBN 9798892328852 (library binding) | ISBN 9798892329156 (ebook)
Subjects: LCSH: Human-alien encounters--Juvenile literature. | Extraterrestrial beings--Juvenile literature.
Classification: LCC BF2050 .W435 2025 (print) | LCC BF2050 (ebook) | DDC 001.942--dc23/eng/20240904
LC record available at https://lccn.loc.gov/2024034992
LC ebook record available at https://lccn.loc.gov/2024034993

For more information, write to Bearport Publishing, 5357 Penn Avenue South, Minneapolis, MN 55419.

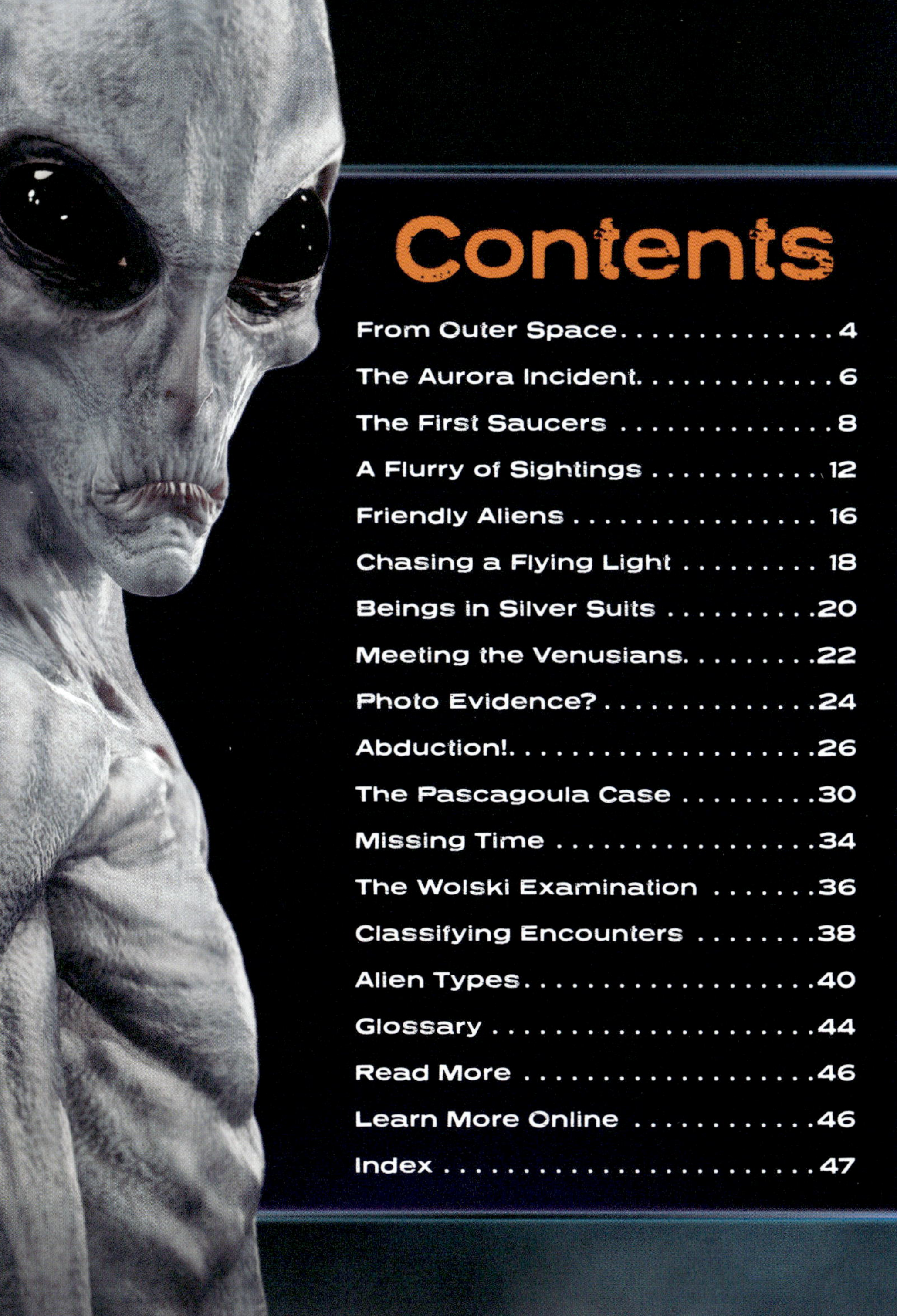

Contents

From Outer Space

Stories of unidentified flying objects, or UFOs, have fascinated humans for decades, spanning cultures and continents. The sightings can defy conventional explanation and range from simple glowing orbs to intricate, structured ships. Reports by witnesses describing direct contact with extraterrestrial beings leave us with an even larger burning question: Are we alone in the universe?

During the period between 1948 and 1969, the United States Air Force investigated 12,618 reported UFO sightings. The vast majority of the sightings were found to have been the result of witnesses seeing human-made objects, weather events, or astronomical phenomena. However, a total of 701 sightings remain unexplained.

The Aurora Incident

One of the first documented cases of an alien encounter comes from Texas. A newspaper article written about the incident in April 1897 tells the story. There had been sightings of what were described as airships near the town of Aurora in the spring of that year. On April 17, witnesses said one of the airships descended and then crashed into a judge's windmill before bursting into flames. The locals said the pilot of the craft was an alien who died in the crash. They speculated he had come from Mars.

Witnesses said the badly wrecked ship was made of an unknown metal that looked like a mixture of aluminum and silver. Some say residents gathered up pieces of the strange metal. The people of Aurora gave the deceased alien a funeral before burying his body in the local cemetery. The remains of the ship were said to have been dumped into a well near the damaged windmill.

In 1935, Brawley Oates purchased the property formerly owned by the local judge. Oates claimed he cleaned out the debris from the well so it could be used as a source of water. Soon after, he developed a very severe case of arthritis, which he claimed was from water that had been contaminated by the pieces of the alien spacecraft. In 1945, Oates sealed up the well with a concrete slab and built a small building over it.

Over the years, there have been numerous investigations into the incident. Some people believe the newspaper article was written as a hoax, designed to bring attention to the small town. Others believe that the event really did happen, pointing to the testimony from witnesses who had been children in Aurora at the time. One investigation requested permission to dig up a grave marked by a stone with a strange carving of a spaceship on it. The commission that oversees Aurora Cemetery declined.

A Windmill Demolishes It.

Aurora, Wise Co., Tex.,Ap ril 17.—(To The News.)—About 6 o'clock this morning the early risers of Aurora were astonished at the sudden appearance of the airship which has been sailing through the country.

It was traveling due north, and much nearer the earth than ever before. Evidently some of the machinery was out of order, for it was making a speed of only ten or twelve miles an hour and gradually settling toward the earth. It sailed directly over the public square, and when it reached the north part of town collided with the tower of Judge Proctor's windmill and went to pieces with a terrific explosion, scattering debris over several acres of ground, wrecking the windmill and water tank and destroying the judge's flower garden.

The pilot of the ship is supposed to have been the only one on board, and while his remains are badly disfigured, enough of the original has been picked up to show that he was not an inhabitant of this world.

Mr. T. J. Weems, the United States signal service officer at this place and an authority on astronomy, gives it as his opinion that he was a native of the planet Mars.

Papers found on his person—evidently the record of his travels—are written in some unknown hieroglyphics, and can not be deciphered.

The ship was too badly wrecked to form any conclusion as to its construction or motive power. It was built of an unknown metal, resembling somewhat a mixture of aluminum and silver, and it must have weighed several tons.

The town is full of people to-day who are viewing the wreck and gathering specimens of the strange metal from the debris. The pilot's funeral will take place at noon to-morrow. S. E. HAYDON.

The article from *The Dallas Morning News*, dated April 19, 1897, describes the pilot of the ship: "While his remains are badly disfigured, enough of the original has been picked up to show that he was not of this world."

A tombstone in Aurora Cemetery has a carving of a spacecraft.

The First Saucers

Kenneth Arnold next to his plane

On June 24, 1947, experienced pilot Kenneth Arnold took off from Chehalis, Washington, in a single-engine airplane heading to an air show in Oregon. On the trip, he had planned to search for a U.S. Marine transport plane that had recently crashed, hoping to claim the $5,000 reward for its discovery. He spent an hour or so flying above the forests around Mount Rainier not far from Seattle, Washington, looking for the downed aircraft. Shortly before 3:00 p.m., Arnold saw a bright flash in the sky.

The pilot was startled, but he assumed what he had seen was just a reflection of the sun on the wings of a military plane he spotted in the distance. However, that plane was heading away from Arnold, and soon there was a second flash farther to the north. When he looked, he saw a line of aircraft flying toward him. As they got closer, Arnold counted nine objects arranged in a military echelon formation, with one craft in the lead and each of the remaining positioned behind and to the side of the one in front of it. He estimated the formation was about 5 miles (8 km) wide.

Although Arnold described the objects as circular without surface markings, a drawing was published a few years after the incident that depicted the objects as crescent-shaped with a dark oval on top. Arnold's photo appeared next to the drawing along with the words, "The Flying Saucer as I Saw it . . . by Kenneth Arnold."

The pilot later described each of the objects as shaped like a flattened circle about 100 feet (30 m) across and said that they occasionally flipped and weaved from side to side, catching sunlight in the process. Each craft appeared to have a highly polished, silver-blue surface with no markings that Arnold could see. He timed the passage of the aircraft formation between two nearby mountains to calculate their speed somewhere between 1,200 and 1,700 miles per hour (1,930 and 2,740 kph)—more than twice that of any known aircraft at the time. The mysterious objects were soon out of sight.

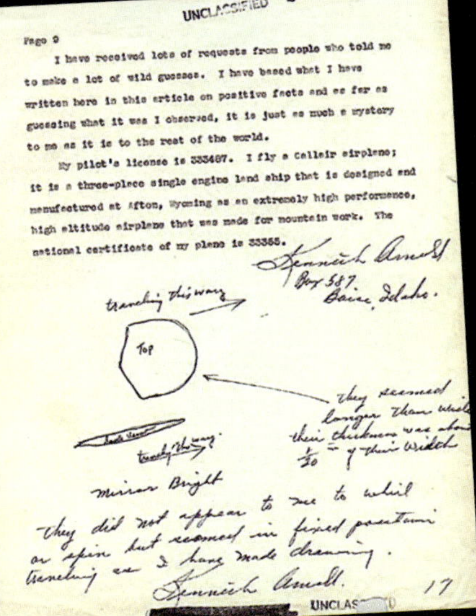

UNCLASSIFIED

Page 9

I have received lots of requests from people who told me to make a lot of wild guesses. I have based what I have written here in this article on positive facts and as far as guessing what it was I observed, it is just as much a mystery to me as it is to the rest of the world.

My pilot's license is 333487. I fly a Callair airplane; it is a three-place single engine land ship that is designed and manufactured at Afton, Wyoming as an extremely high performance, high altitude airplane that was made for mountain work. The national certificate of my plane is 33355.

Kenneth Arnold
Box 587
Boise, Idaho.

traveling this way

Top

they seemed longer than wide their thickness was about 1/20 of their width

traveling this way

mirror Bright

they did not appear to me to whirl or spin but seemed in fixed position traveling as I have made drawing.

Kenneth Arnold.

17

UNCLAS[illegible]

A typed letter by Kenneth Arnold to an Air Force general describing what he had seen, with added handwritten notes and drawings

Arnold headed to nearby Yakima Airfield to refuel and then went to see Al Baxter, a general manager of Central Aircraft. The two men discussed the sighting, and Arnold drew pictures of what he had seen. Other pilots and crew joined the conversation, but none could explain the mysterious aircraft other than to guess that they were part of a secret military project. Arnold resumed his flight to Oregon.

The next day, Arnold stopped by at the office of the local newspaper, the *East Oregonian*, to find out if the military had been testing secret warplanes in the area. He spoke with reporter Bill Bequette, who—years later—said the pilot seemed "honest, level-headed, and credible" as a witness. Bequette wrote

According to newspapers at the time, Captain E. J. Smith (*left*) and Kenneth Arnold compared notes on what they had seen.

a short article about Arnold's experience, which was picked up by newspapers around the country. Other articles followed, and soon, people across the United States and around the world knew about the encounter with the mysterious flying objects.

Since Arnold had been concerned that the aircraft could be a threat to national security, he also told his story to the local office of the Federal Bureau of Investigation (FBI) and later to military personnel. The initial FBI report concluded by saying, "It is the personal opinion of the interviewer that Arnold actually saw what he states he saw in the attached report."

The cover of a special edition of *Amazing Stories* magazine published after Arnold's sighting

Kenneth Arnold became famous for his sighting of the nine mysterious objects flying near Mt. Rainier, although he never received the explanation he sought from the government. He also felt that his fame was not entirely positive. Over the next several years, he attempted many times to find the objects again, but without success. He wrote in a 1952 book, "I have been subjected to ridicule [and] much loss of time and money."

News sources at the time cite Arnold as having described the objects using the terms *saucer*, *disk*, and *pie-pan*. However, Arnold strongly denied ever having described the objects as saucer-shaped, but instead compared their motion to "a saucer if you skip it across water." Apparently, newspapers around the country mistakenly understood that to refer to the shape of the objects, and *flying saucer* became the popular term to describe similar sightings and eventually all UFOs.

A Flurry of Sightings

After the story of what Kenneth Arnold saw was published, it spread extremely quickly. The host of a radio interview a few days later said of the story, "It's been on every newscast, over the air, and in every newspaper I know of." It was not long before many other people began coming forward with their own stories of having seen saucer-shaped objects or bright lights moving in unusual ways.

Two Shadows

News of Arnold's sightings prompted some to come forward with stories from years earlier. One report described a group of boys from Baradine, Australia, hunting rabbits by moonlight one night in 1931. One of the boys claimed to have suddenly noticed that he was casting two shadows in the moonlight instead of one. Looking up, he saw a disk-shaped object approaching from the northwest. The group claimed that orange lights or flames slowly flashed and rotated around the rim of the object as it flew. The disk followed a straight course before disappearing behind nearby hills.

Flight 105

On July 4, 1947, as United Airlines Flight 105 took off from Boise, Idaho, air traffic controllers apparently joked that the flight needed to be on the lookout for flying saucers. Eight minutes into the flight, First Officer Ralph Stevens and Captain E. J. Smith spotted something approaching them in the evening sky. The pilots said they saw four or five objects and later described them as flat and circular. According to Smith, each was bigger than the DC-3 aircraft the men were flying.

The objects appeared to fly in a loose formation. Soon, they disappeared. However, the mysterious craft were quickly replaced by four more. Stevens and Smith followed the objects for 10 to 15 minutes, covering about 45 miles (72 km). The pilots radioed a nearby airport and another United flight in the area, but nobody else had reported seeing the objects. Stevens and Smith asked flight attendant Marty Marrow to come to the cockpit, and she later confirmed what the pilots saw. None of the passengers on board, however, had seen the objects.

There are a few reasons that the term *UFO* quickly began to replace *flying saucer* as the preferred way to describe the sightings. First, it was becoming clear that only some of the objects were described as disk-shaped. The new term also lent an air of scientific inquiry to any discussion or report and implied an openness to many interpretations. Today, many people use the term *UAP*, which stands for unidentified aerial phenomena. It has a meaning very similar to that of *UFO*.

The Roswell Incident

Just two weeks after Arnold's sighting, the press officer at Walker Air Force Base in Roswell, New Mexico, issued a dramatic press release. It said a "flying disk" had crashed near the base and that air force personnel were investigating the debris. The press pounced on the story, expecting that the mystery of the UFO would soon be solved. However, shortly afterward, Major Jesse Marcel called a press conference to announce that the crashed saucer was in fact just debris from a weather balloon.

Roswell Daily Record

RAAF Captures Flying Saucer On Ranch in Roswell Region

Claims Army Is Stacking Courts Martial

House Passes Tax Slash by Large Margin

Security Council Paves Way to Talks On Arms Reductions

No Details of Flying Disk Are Revealed

Ex-King Carol Weds Mme. Lupescu

***Roswell Daily Record*, July 8, 1947**

The incident was largely forgotten until 1978, when the original article was reprinted. In an interview, retired Lieutenant Colonel Marcel said he now believes the Roswell debris was extraterrestrial in origin. Several books, TV shows, and interviews further explored the incident, and many people became convinced of a government conspiracy. Today, the Roswell incident is the basis for many extraterrestrial, flying saucer, and government coverup stories.

Major Jesse A. Marcel poses with debris from the Roswell crash during a July 8, 1947, press conference.

Snake River Canyon

Mr. A. C. Urie and his two young sons were on a fishing trip at Snake River Canyon, Idaho, on August 13, 1947. They claimed to have seen a disk flying low over the canyon about 300 ft. (90 m) away. They reported that the object was about 75 ft. (23 m) above the canyon floor and moving extremely fast up and over the hills. The father and sons described the object as about 20 ft. (6 m) long, and about 10 ft. (3 m) both wide and tall. They claimed its shape was like that of a broad-brimmed straw hat and that it made a soft whishing noise as it passed. As it rose out of the canyon, the object flew low over a line of trees, which bent and twisted as if caught in a sudden, violent wind.

An Astronomer's Sighting

Clyde Tombaugh was an astronomer who had discovered the dwarf planet Pluto. On the evening of August 20, 1949, Tombaugh was sitting outside his house in Las Cruces, New Mexico, with his wife and mother-in-law when he saw a green light out of the corner of his eye. According to Tombaugh, when he looked up, he saw seven other lights the same green color and all flying in the same direction. The craft made no sound as they powered overhead and vanished into the distance. Tombaugh said of the incident, "I was so unprepared for such a strange sight that I was really petrified with astonishment."

Lieutenant Colonel Hector Quintanilla (*seated*) with other members of the staff of Project Blue Book

At the end of 1947, the United States Air Force formed Project Sign, a group whose mission was to explore UFOs. A few years later, the group was replaced by Project Grudge, and then in 1952 the group finally became Project Blue Book. From 1952 until 1969, the project collected, filed, and analyzed many thousands of reports of UFO sightings to provide scientific oversight as well as to determine possible threats to national security.

Friendly Aliens

In 1940, Udo Wartena was a miner working part-time for Northwest Mining Company near Townsend, Montana. Many years later, he shared an extraordinary story of an encounter with an alien being. Wartena said that one morning in early May, he was at the base of Boulder Mountain clearing some rocks near a stream when he heard a humming sound. He first took the noise to be an airplane from a nearby base, but when it continued longer than usual, Wartena became curious. He climbed to higher ground to get a closer look.

Wartena claimed that hovering above a meadow was a large disc-shaped object about 100 ft. (30 m) wide and 35 ft. (11 m) tall. He described it as a dull steel color and shaped like two plates, one on top of the other. The miner reported that as he stood watching, a circular stairway came down from the craft and a man descended the stairs and walked toward him. The man was wearing light gray coveralls with a circular cap of the same material, and he began to speak.

According to Wartena, the man shook his hand and apologized, saying they had not known anyone was in the area, and he explained that their custom was not to interrupt or allow themselves to be seen. The stranger asked Wartena if he could take water from the stream. After Wartena agreed, the man gave a signal to the object, and a hose was lowered into the running water. The man reportedly asked Wartena if he would like to come aboard the ship, and after agreeing, they went up the stairs and into the object.

Wartena said he found himself in a room about 12 by 15 ft. (3.7 by 4.6 m) with padded benches on the sides. In the room, Wartena spotted another man who was plainly dressed, with snow-white hair and nearly transparent skin. Wartena said that when he asked about their ages, one claimed to be about 600 years old, and the other more than 900 years old, according to how they measured time.

The conversation continued, according to Wartena, with the men explaining their reasons for visiting Earth, including things like gathering information and providing help. They claimed they were from another planet and said their ship moved by manipulating gravity and focusing on the energies of distant stars. Soon, Wartena realized it was time to go and left the ship. He reported watching the craft rise straight up and quickly disappear out of sight. Wartena said that after the craft left, he lost strength in his body and was unable to walk for several hours.

Years after the incident, Wartena told a family member why the aliens had taken water from the stream. He claimed the men told him they wanted to extract hydrogen from the water to use as a fuel source. Hydrogen is the element in the sun that generates the star's enormous energy. NASA and other space agencies around the world have long used hydrogen to make rocket fuel.

Chasing a Flying Light

Lieutenant George Gorman was a former fighter pilot working for the North Dakota Air National Guard near the city of Fargo in 1948. Around 9 p.m. on October 1, Gorman was flying over a lit football stadium, about to end a routine practice flight in a P-51 fighter. At an altitude of about 4,600 ft. (1,400 m), the pilot suddenly saw a flash of light below that he thought was the taillight of another plane. After confirming with the air traffic tower that the only other aircraft was a Piper Cub that Gorman could see to the west, he decided to take a closer look.

Gorman flew his plane to within 3,000 ft. (900 m) of the flying light, which he described as a clear-white color between 6 and 8 inches (15 to 20 cm) in diameter. In his report, he wrote, "It was blinking on and off. As I approached, however, the light suddenly became steady and pulled into a sharp left bank." Thinking that the light was heading for the tower, Gorman decided to follow. The pilot was finally able to catch up with the light at an altitude of about 7,000 ft. (2,100 m) when the light made a sharp turn and headed straight for Gorman. Just as it was about to hit his plane, Gorman dived and the light shot above him before turning sharply again in his direction. Just as the light was about to make contact, it shot straight up in the air in a steep climb. When Gorman tried to follow, his plane stalled at about 14,000 ft. (4,300 m), and he was forced to return to land.

Gorman was shaken by the encounter. He reported that there had been no sound or exhaust trail from the object. Although he had reached speeds of 400 mph (640 kph), he had been unable to catch the mysterious light. Despite Gorman being in good physical condition, he also reported blacking out temporarily due to the excessive speed. He had been shocked at how the object had been able to turn so much more easily and fly so much faster than his airplane.

Gorman wasn't the only witness to the mysterious object that night. Air traffic controllers Lloyd D. Jenson and H. E. Johnson were working at Hector Airport, and both reported seeing the Piper Cub plane and the flying light at the same time. The pilot and passenger of the Piper Cub as well as two airport workers on the ground also saw the object. All of the other stories matched Gorman's descriptions of the shape, size, and speed of the object.

Beings in Silver Suits

In 1952, near the town of Hasselbach, Germany, Oscar Linke and his 11-year-old daughter, Gabriella, were on their way home. Linke's motorcycle had gotten a flat, and the two were walking when Gabriella pointed to something in the distance. In the evening light, Linke thought his daughter was pointing to a young deer near the woods. He leaned his motorcycle against a nearby tree and walked toward where Gabriella had pointed. Linke realized his first impression had been wrong. Instead of a deer, he saw two men dressed in what seemed to be metallic clothing and who were looking at something lying on the ground.

Linke moved closer, and as he peered over a small fence, he saw a large, round metal object that resembled a huge frying pan. He estimated it was 45 to 50 ft. (14 to 15 m) across. The object had two rows of holes running along its edge, with a black, cone-shaped tower sticking up about 10 ft. (3 m) out of the top. One of the men had a light on the front part of his body, which lit up at regular intervals. Gabriella was a short distance behind her father, and when she called out to him, the men in the silver suits immediately jumped onto the tower and disappeared inside.

The holes on the side of the ship began to light up, brighter and brighter, first turning a green color then changing to red. Linke and his daughter could hear a loud humming noise, and the object began to rise slowly. There seemed to be a ring of flames around the now-hovering object, and it rose higher off the ground with a strange whistling sound. The object then flew over the forest in the direction of a nearby city.

Many other people in the area also reported seeing an object that evening, most thinking it had been a comet. Linke stated later, "I would have thought that both my daughter and I were dreaming . . . [but] . . . when the object had disappeared, I went to the place where it had been. I found a circular opening in the ground . . . exactly the same shape as the conical tower. I was then convinced that I was not dreaming."

In response to the events of World War II (1939–1945), the United States created the Foreign Broadcast Information Service to collect and record any public radio broadcasts from foreign countries. At the same time, the CIA was secretly also collecting foreign broadcasts, as well as any written documents important to national security. Linke's story was found in one of the CIA's secret documents that were made available to the public many years later.

Meeting the Venusians

In 1954, George Adamski shot to international fame with the publication of his book *Flying Saucers Have Landed*. The book, co-written by his friend Desmond Leslie, was based on Adamski's reported encounter with a UFO two years earlier. Adamski claimed he met and communicated with a visitor from Venus.

Flying Saucers Have Landed
Desmond Leslie & George Adamski

According to Adamski, he had seen UFOs in 1946, 1947, and 1949. He claimed that by 1952, he had taken more than 500 flying saucer photographs but that only a dozen or so were clear images. In November of that year, Adamski said he and some friends were enjoying a picnic in a California desert when they saw a large, cigar-shaped UFO pass overhead, followed quickly by military jets chasing after. He claimed a smaller disk-shaped object detached itself and landed a mile (1.6 km) or so away. While his friends waited, Adamski set off to investigate.

George Adamski claimed these photographs were evidence that alien spacecraft had visited Earth. Many believed he faked the images using common objects and lighting effects.

George Adamski in front of a painting of the Venusian he claimed to have met

As he approached the landed craft, he claimed he was met by a humanoid with long, glistening hair dressed in brown coveralls. The alien did not speak but made himself understood by a mixture of hand signals and telepathy. The being explained that he had come from Venus as a messenger to Earth to warn about the dangers of nuclear bombs and their risk to the entire planet. The Venusian explained that beings from Jupiter, Saturn, and other planets would resort to force if humans did not change their ways.

Adamski claimed that he was visited by the Venusians several more times and in fact had been taken to the moon and to Venus, where he found lush forests. While many did not believe his stories, Adamski went on to write two other best-selling flying saucer books. He also traveled widely to lecture on the subject.

Despite the outlandish nature of Adamski's claims, apparently some famous people believed them. Queen Juliana of the Netherlands was very interested in the subjects of UFOs and aliens and invited Adamski to visit in 1959. Adamski also claimed to have had a secret meeting with Pope John XXIII in 1963, during which he received a golden medal.

Photo Evidence?

On January 16, 1958, the Brazilian survey ship *Almirante Saldanha* was at a naval base on the island of Trindade, located in the Atlantic Ocean about 750 miles (1,200 km) off the east coast of Brazil. The ship was on an assignment to take underwater photographs near the remote island, and photographer Almiro Baraúna claimed to have seen and photographed a disk-shaped flying ship over the island. He described his story in a letter written several years later.

Photograph by Almiro Baraúna of an alleged flying saucer over Trindade Island, 1958

Were Baraúna's photos a hoax? Some people think so. Several of the details in Baraúna's letter seem to be inaccurate, such as the number of other witnesses who saw the flying craft. According to the captain of the boat, only about eight people had seen anything at all. There were also several allegations over the years that Baraúna had faked the photos entirely. People claim that when he made the enlargements, he used parts of another photo he had taken of two spoons put together to look like a spacecraft.

Baraúna wrote that around 11 a.m. he was on deck when a group of people at the back of the ship sounded an alarm. Everyone on the deck—about 50 people—saw a "strange silver plate-shaped object, which was moving from the sea towards the island." Baraúna said the object did not make any noise and moved in rising and falling motions, sometimes quickly and other times more slowly. When the object increased its speed, it left behind a glowing white trail that soon faded away. Baraúna claimed they saw the object move behind a hill on the island, then quickly reappear on the same side of the hill before disappearing into the distance.

While the object was still in view, Baraúna was able to take four photos. Because photographic film was used at the time, it needed to be developed using chemical baths in a darkened lab. They used a room on the ship, and Baraúna said that at the request of the ship's commander, the film was developed about 20 minutes after the sighting and that the negatives were seen by nearly the entire crew. Since the photographic equipment on board was limited, they had to wait until the ship was back on shore to make enlargements of the photographs. The photos and story made international news.

Abduction!

In September 1961, Betty and Barney Hill were driving late at night along a country road through the White Mountains in New Hampshire. They were returning home to Portsmouth after a three-day trip and decided to travel at night to avoid some approaching bad weather. They hadn't seen another car for miles when suddenly they noticed a strange light in the sky.

At first, the light looked like a falling star. But it seemed to grow brighter and larger as they drove. Perhaps more oddly, it appeared to be following them. The light sometimes disappeared behind trees or mountain ridges, only to reappear soon afterward. The couple became curious and pulled off the road to get a better look. Through binoculars, Betty saw that the object had flashing lights and was spinning in the air. When Barney looked through the binoculars, he thought it looked like a commercial airliner except that it made sharp turns in their direction.

The Hills continued their trip as the silent craft bounced along in the sky following them. Soon, the object descended rapidly, causing the couple to stop the car in the middle of the road. The huge craft hovered 50 to 80 ft. (15 to 24 m) above them. Barney claimed that through the binoculars, he saw 8 to 11 humanlike figures watching them from windows. He said they were dressed in glossy dark uniforms and caps.

When the Hills arrived home, they tried to make sense of the strange experience. They had both felt odd sensations and drew pictures of what they had seen. Their watches had stopped and never worked again. There were shiny, concentric circles on the trunk of their car that had not been there before. When the couple tried to reconstruct the event, their memories felt incomplete and fragmented. Betty and Barney soon realized that they couldn't account for several hours of their trip.

The Hills reported their experience to the United States Air Force as well as to the National Investigations Committee on Aerial Phenomena (NICAP), a group that documented such stories from the 1950s to the 1980s. The couple was considered to be credible, but neither the Air Force nor the NICAP was able to explain the incident.

An illustration of meeting the spaceship based on descriptions provided by the Hills

In the months and years after the incident, Betty had disturbing dreams and Barney developed anxiety and an ulcer. The couple sought help and met with Dr. Benjamin Simon, a psychiatrist and neurologist who specialized in hypnosis, a common treatment at the time. In weekly sessions over several months, the couple and Dr. Simon were able to piece together what they think happened during the missing time on that night in 1961.

The details of Betty's dreams and of both Betty's and Barney's hypnosis sessions largely agreed. The Hills had pulled off the road and driven a bit into the woods. The car stalled and they saw three or more beings take them into a spacecraft. The Hills were separated once inside the ship.

Betty and Barney recalled sitting on metal tables in examination rooms with curved walls and lights in the ceiling. The couple said the aliens took strands of hair, nail clippings, and skin scrapings and placed the samples on a clear material. The beings used needles with long wires connected to them to probe their heads, legs, arms, and spines. They seemed to communicate with the Hills without words, using what Barney described as thought transference. Betty was able to recall having been shown a star map on the ship.

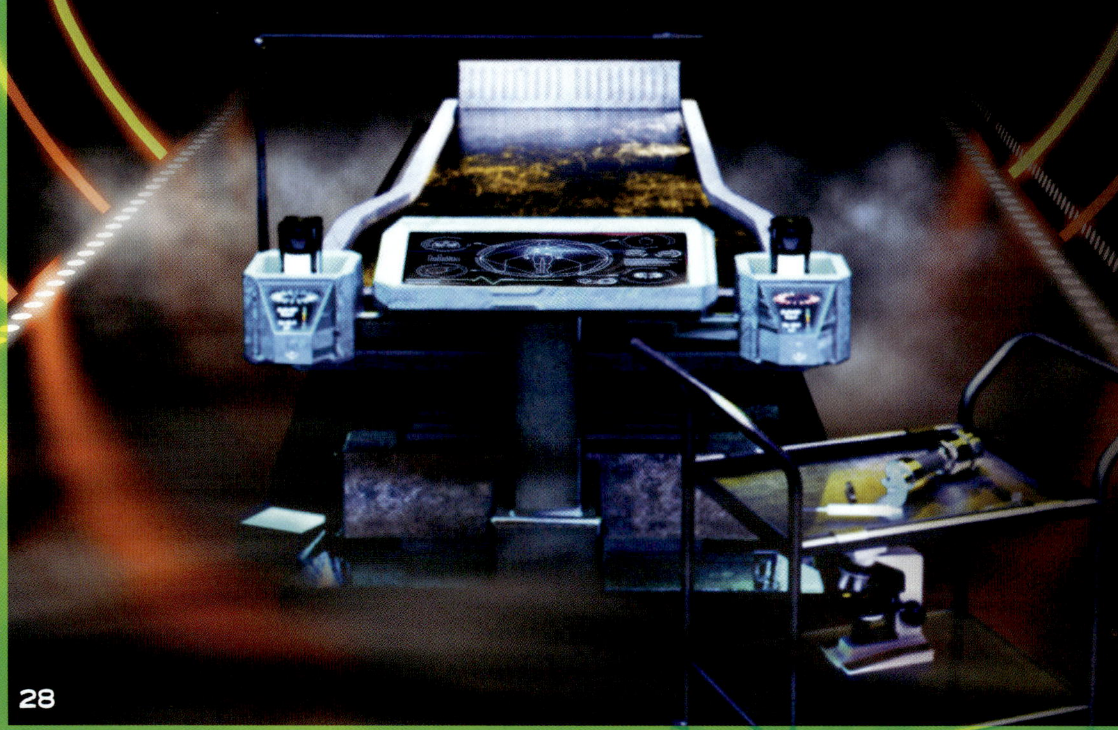

Betty and Barney Hill holding a newspaper with an article about their encounter

The Hills continued with their private life and apparently did not make any effort to seek publicity. However, in 1965 a newspaper called the *Boston Traveller* ran a front-page story entitled "UFO Chiller: Did THEY Seize Couple?" This article led to others, and soon the Hills' abduction story became world-famous. The following year, John G. Fuller wrote a hugely successful book about the Hills' experience entitled *The Interrupted Journey*.

Hypnotherapy, also known as hypnotic medicine, is a therapeutic practice that uses guided hypnosis to help a person enter a trancelike state of focus. While it is accepted as an effective method to manage pain and achieve desired behavior changes, many people doubt it is a way to recover accurate memories.

The Pascagoula Case

On the evening of October 11, 1973, two shipyard workers ran into the county sheriff's office in Pascagoula, Mississippi, to report an extraordinary encounter. They said they had been abducted by aliens. Charlie Hickson and Calvin Parker claimed they had been fishing off a pier on the west side of the Pascagoula River when they heard a whirring sound. Then, they noticed a blue light reflecting in the water and thought the police had come to ask them to leave the area. Instead, the men said, an oval-shaped object appeared from behind the clouds.

In interviews years later, the men said the object was glowing blue and estimated it was about 80 ft. (24 m) wide. The object was reportedly hovering about 3 ft. (1 m) off the ground when a door on the side of the craft opened and three humanlike creatures floated out. Parker described the creatures as about 5 ft. (1.5 m) tall, with a single leg ending in a footlike appendage without toes. Their domed heads had slits for mouths and small ears that stuck out from the sides. Their hands were described as shaped like mittens or crab claws. Both Parker and Hickson said they had the impression that the creatures were robots rather than living beings.

The Pascagoula encounter caused the largest renewal of interest in UFOs and alien abductions since Betty and Barney Hill's story years earlier. In the two weeks following Hickson and Parker's experience, hundreds of other UFO sightings were reported to Mississippi authorities.

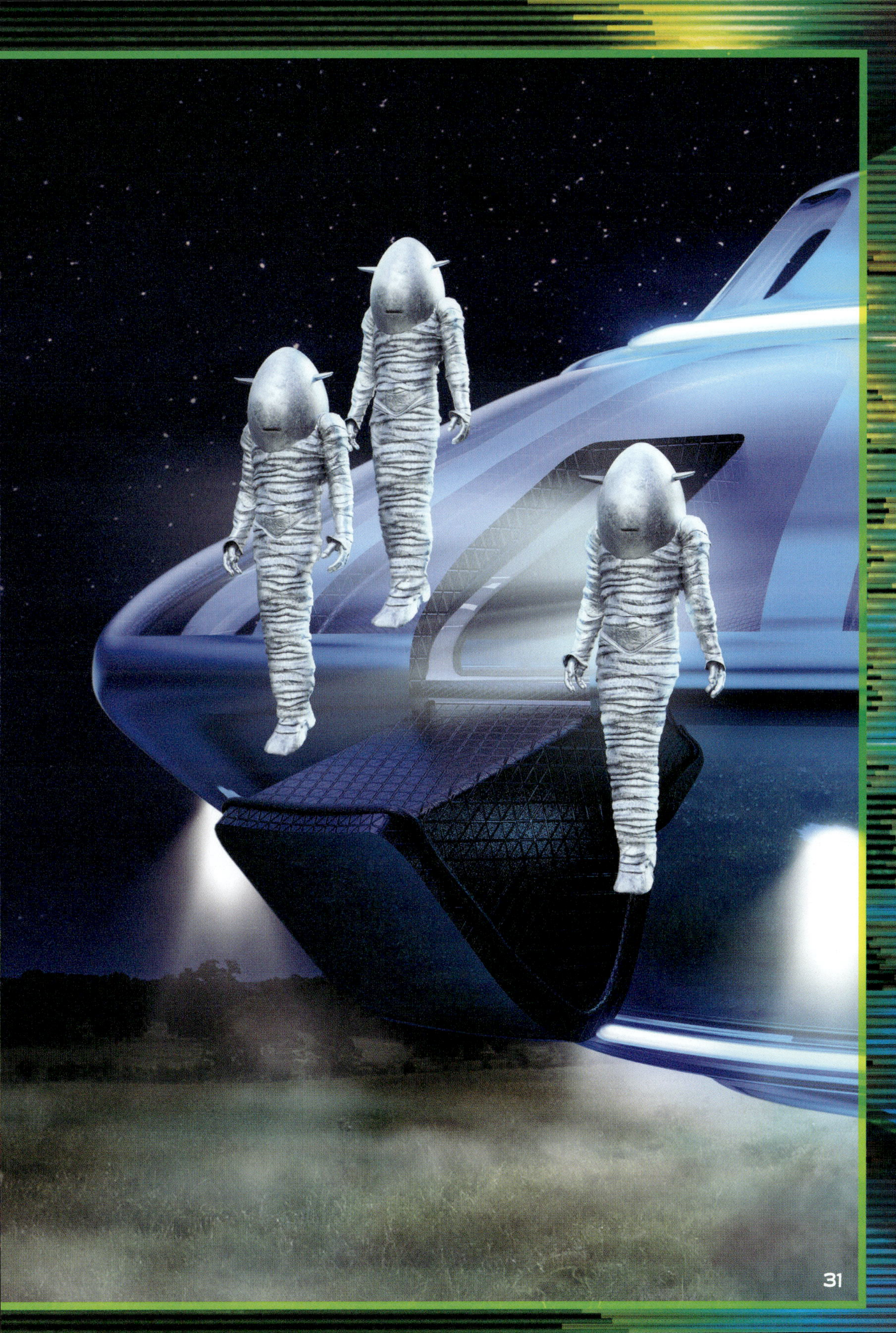

Parker said he was terrified, but that one of the beings put one of its claws around his arm and he suddenly calmed down. He thought perhaps he had been injected with something and described feeling numb afterward. The two men claimed the aliens brought them into the spacecraft. Hickson said, "When I got in . . . there were no seats, no chain, they just moved me around. I couldn't resist them. I just floated, felt no sensation, no pain." He also described a machine he thought was used for medical examinations. "It looked like an eye, like a big eye. It had some kind of an attachment to it. It moved . . . all over my body, up and down."

During the interviews, the men said they couldn't recall exactly how they found themselves back on the riverbank near where they had been fishing. At first, they were dazed and thought it might be best never to tell anyone about their encounter. But they then changed their minds and headed to the sheriff's office to report the incident.

In 2020, recordings of Parker and Hickson being interviewed by the sheriff were sent to Parker by an unnamed officer of the Pascagoula Police Department. While the men had been speaking with the sheriff that night in 1973, a hidden recording device had captured everything they said. At one point, the sheriff had stepped out of the room and left Parker and Hickson alone. The recording documented the two men talking about being afraid, needing sleep, and wanting to see a doctor. Here are some quotes from that portion of the recording:

PARKER: I got to get home and get to bed or . . . or see the doctor or something. I can't stand it. I'm about to go half crazy.

HICKSON: I tell you, when we're through, I'll get you something to settle you down so you can get some . . . sleep.

PARKER: My arms, I remember they just froze up and I couldn't move. Just like I stepped on a . . . rattlesnake. . . . I passed out. I expect I never passed out in my whole life.

HICKSON: I've never seen nothin' like that before in my life. You can't make people believe.

PARKER: I don't want to keep sittin' here. I want to see a doctor.

HICKSON: They better wake up and start believin' . . . they better start believin'.

After the interview, the sheriff arranged for Parker and Hickson to have a medical examination at a nearby Air Force base. The doctor there found no signs of injuries or radiation, though both men did have small cuts similar to those caused by taking blood samples. Hickson also took and passed a lie detector test. The incident attracted lots of publicity. Hickson gave interviews and appeared on television. In 1983, he wrote a book about his experience. In 2018, after many years of silence, Parker also wrote a book describing how the events affected his life.

Professors Dr. James Hardler (*left*) and Dr. J. Allen Hynek questioned Parker and Hickson about their experience in the alien spacecraft. Both scientists said they believed the men's story.

In June 2019, a local society placed a historical marker near the location of the 1973 Pascagoula events as described by Charles Hickson and Calvin Parker. Hickson died in 2011, but his family attended the unveiling, as did Parker. At the ceremony, Parker said, "It is emotional for me. I can't really describe it because I would break out in tears if I do. . . . It is quite an honor."

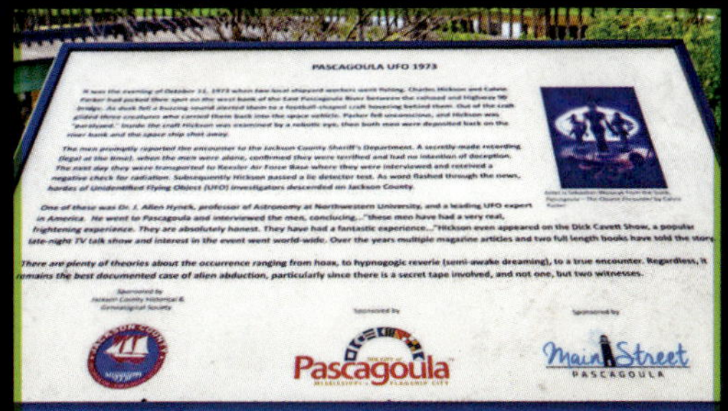

Missing Time

On the evening of October 27, 1974, John and Sue Day were driving home in Essex, England, with their three children sleeping in the back seat. The Days were hoping to be back in time for a television program they wanted to watch. According to reports, as the Days were driving, they saw an oval-shaped blue light in the sky that seemed to be following them. After a while, the car quickly became engulfed by a dense greenish mist. The car radio began to buzz with static and emit smoke, so John quickly disconnected it. Suddenly, there was a jolt as if their car had run over an object. The mist was gone, and the startled family continued their drive home.

Once at their house, John reconnected the car radio and Sue took the children indoors and put them to bed. When Sue went back downstairs to turn on the television show, she was not able to find it. Soon, she glanced at a clock and was astonished to see that it was almost midnight, nearly three hours later than it should have been. John, too, was shocked and couldn't explain the strange lapse in time. The couple went to bed exhausted.

In the weeks that followed, the family began to have strange dreams with recurring images of monstrous faces. Both John and Sue found themselves becoming increasingly focused on environmental issues, which had interested them very little before. The family became vegetarians and adopted a healthier lifestyle. Eventually, the nightmares got to be too much, and the Days went to see Dr. Leonard Wilder, a specialist in trauma and sleep disorders. Dr. Wilder hypnotized both John and Sue to dig up their memories of the night in question.

In UFO stories, missing time is common. It refers to a sudden, unexplained gap in memory following a UFO sighting or encounter. Individuals experiencing this phenomenon are left disoriented, unable to recall events during the lost time that may last minutes or hours. Later, under hypnosis or deep recollection, they often describe being taken aboard an alien craft and interacting with extraterrestrial beings.

In the sessions, John and Sue recalled nearly identical tales. When their car had entered the green mist, the engine died completely. Then, they saw a group of aliens dressed in tight-fitting silver suits. They were more than 6 ft. (1.8 m) tall and humanlike in appearance, except for penetrating, catlike eyes. The aliens escorted the couple from their car through the mist and onto the blue UFO. Once inside, the Days were handed over to a different group of aliens. They were shorter, standing at about 4 ft. (1.2 m) tall, and had animallike faces with large eyes and pointed ears. The Days realized it was these faces that had been haunting their dreams.

Each of the Days was then examined in turn by the smaller aliens. Once the tests were over, the taller aliens reappeared. They showed the family around the UFO and told the Days that Earth was in danger of devastation by pollution and other environmental threats. The Days had the impression that the aliens had been visiting and studying humans for a long time. The Days then recalled being led back out of the UFO and through the mist to their car. John started the engine and they set off for home.

The Wolski Examination

On May 10, 1978, Jan Wolski, a farmer from Emilcin, Poland, claimed to have had a remarkable encounter. While driving his horse-drawn cart through the quiet countryside, Wolski said two small, humanoid figures jumped aboard. These beings, about 5 ft. (1.5 m) tall, had greenish skin and slanted eyes. Their movements were fluid, and they communicated in an unknown language using odd sounds and gestures. The beings led him to a clearing where a large, white craft hovered about 16 ft. (5 m) above the ground. There was a sort of elevator extending from an open hatch. Wolski followed the beings onto the elevator, which rose up into the ship.

Inside, Wolski found himself in a windowless, sterile room with nothing but bare walls and a few benches. The beings directed Wolski to undress and lie down on a table that resembled a medical examination bed. Without speaking, they used instruments that resembled two saucers to conduct a painless examination. The beings then offered Wolski some strange honey-like food, but he politely declined.

After the examination, the beings allowed Wolski to dress, and they escorted him back to the elevator. He went down a ramp and returned to his cart. The beings waved at him before the elevator moved upward and they ascended into the craft. The ship then rose silently into the sky, disappearing from sight within seconds.

Upon returning to his village, Wolski immediately told his family and neighbors what had happened, and together they went to investigate the site. News of Wolski's story quickly spread, drawing the attention of local and international UFO investigators. Wolski underwent several interviews and a polygraph test, which he passed, adding credibility to his account. Within months of the incident, a documentary film shared Wolski's story. In the years that followed, several books also reported on the event.

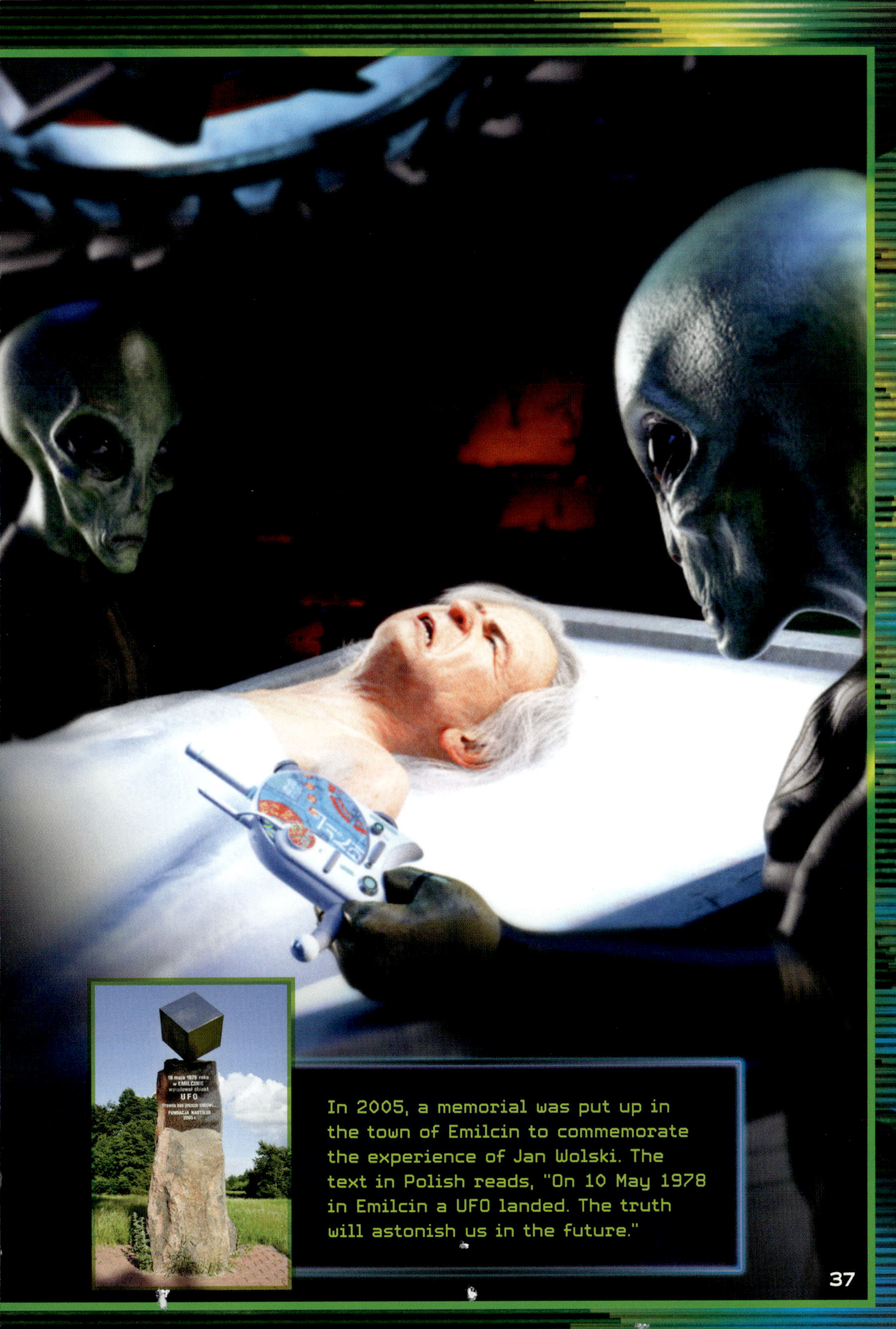

In 2005, a memorial was put up in the town of Emilcin to commemorate the experience of Jan Wolski. The text in Polish reads, "On 10 May 1978 in Emilcin a UFO landed. The truth will astonish us in the future."

Classifying Encounters

Joseph Allen Hynek was an astronomer and professor, initially skeptical of stories of alien encounters. However, Hynek's involvement with Project Blue Book led him to take UFO reports more seriously. His work eventually led to the creation of a systematic way to categorize UFO sightings, known as the Hynek Classification System. The system divided sightings at distances of 500 ft. (150 m) or more into two categories: Nocturnal Lights or Daylight Discs, depending on the time of day when they occurred. For events in which witnesses were nearer to the UFOs, Hynek described three categories of what he termed Close Encounters.

J. Allen Hynek's UFO encounter classification system was designed to provide a structured way to analyze and report sightings.

Some people believe crop circles are evidence of UFO landings.

Nocturnal Lights involve lights seen in the night sky. They often move in unusual ways, unlike conventional aircraft or natural phenomena. This category includes a wide range of observations, from simple points of light to complex patterns of movement.

Daylight Discs are sightings that occur during the daytime and involve objects clearly visible to the observer. The term *disc* refers to the common shape reported, though other shapes are also included. These objects are often described as metallic and can move at incredible speeds or hover silently.

Close Encounters of the First Kind: These involve sightings of an unidentified flying object within 500 ft. (150 m), providing a good amount of detail. There is no interaction between the UFO and the environment or the observer.

Close Encounters of the Second Kind: In these cases, the UFO interacts with the environment. This can include physical effects, such as scorch marks on the ground, damaged vegetation, or interference with electronic devices.

Close Encounters of the Third Kind: These encounters involve sightings of occupants or beings associated with the UFO. This category gained widespread fame with the popular 1977 film *Close Encounters of the Third Kind*, which was in part inspired by Hynek's work.

Hynek's work helped legitimize the study of UFOs and encouraged others to approach the subject with a more open and scientific mindset. After his death in 1986, his colleague Jacques Vallee extended the classification system. A close encounter of the fourth kind involves any event in which a human is abducted by a UFO or its occupants. A fifth kind is where a human who had been abducted has some remaining physical effect, such as evidence of an injury. Later the fifth kind was adapted to sometimes include communication with extraterrestrial life forms.

Alien Types

Researchers who have studied eyewitness accounts of UFOs and the descriptions of aliens have found that there are many similarities. The reported aliens usually fit into one of several types.

Grays

Researchers say the most common type of reported alien is the gray. According to witnesses, these aliens are just under 4 ft. (1.2 m) tall and are humanoid in appearance. They have thin arms, legs, and bodies but have large, rounded heads. The arms and legs are sometimes said to lack elbows or knees and to end in long fingers and toes without clearly defined joints.

The grays' heads are hairless without visible ears or noses, and their mouths are often described as small slits. The eyes of gray aliens are almost always described as being extremely large, black, and almond-shaped. Some witnesses felt that the eyes had hypnotic or telepathic powers.

Gray aliens are generally reported as unfriendly. They are said to try to take humans onto their spacecraft for a variety of purposes.

Gray aliens are also sometimes known as Zeta Reticulans, named from the binary star system more than 39 light-years from Earth. Grays became associated with this system because of the alien abduction story of Betty and Barney Hill. Under hypnosis, Betty claimed to have been shown a map of her abductors' home planet and star system. She later redrew that map and it was interpreted as depicting the Zeta Reticuli system.

Nordic Aliens

Nordic aliens were given this name since they've been described as humanlike and tall, with long blond hair and blue eyes. Reports generally say they are dressed in one-piece, tight outfits similar to ski suits or motorcycle gear. These aliens are reported to behave in an aloof or detached fashion and are said to stare at the humans who see them. Some reports even claim the aliens appear to take notes or discuss the humans they're observing. Some witnesses describe Nordic aliens as friendly. This type of alien was reported most frequently during the 1950s and 1960s.

Goblin Type

UFO experts say goblin aliens are short in stature, usually around 3 to 4 ft. (0.9 to 1.2 m) tall. While reports describe this type of alien as having two arms, one head, and walking upright on two legs, they are also described as very bizarre in appearance. According to some witnesses, their long arms end in claws or talons, and they have pointed ears and evil-looking eyes on their large heads. Some goblin aliens are said to be covered in dense fur, while others are described as having smooth or reptilian skin. Some reports indicate that goblin aliens attack humans by cutting and scratching them and that they sometimes even attempt to drag people into their spacecraft. Reported sightings of goblin types have been rare.

Tricksters

Another commonly seen alien is the trickster type. According to witnesses, trickster aliens are like humans in appearance, though they rarely stand more than 3 ft. (0.9 m) tall. They are often said to wear one-piece suits, sometimes with helmets or face masks. Trickster aliens are frequently reported to be deeply interested in plants and animals, especially crops and domestic livestock. Some claim to have seen trickster aliens taking samples of plants and attempting to trap animals. It seems that trickster aliens are mostly uninterested in humans, and they seemingly appear bothered by the arrival of one. Some reports claim trickster aliens use a beam of light to freeze or incapacitate any humans they encounter.

Robots, Blobs, And More

In addition to humanoid aliens, other types have reportedly been seen. Robots are the most numerous of these non-humanlike beings. Reports describe the robots in various shapes and with a metallic appearance, often with flashing lights attached to their bodies. Some people have claimed that the robots were able to shoot a laser at them. Some researchers say people have seen aliens described in a wide variety of other forms, including disembodied brains, headless birdmen, or bouncing blobs of jelly. Most sightings of these types of aliens have been unique occurrences, without others reporting having seen similar beings.

The 1951 movie *The Day the Earth Stood Still* was the story of an alien visitor to Earth. The humanoid alien, named Klaatu, was accompanied by a powerful robot named Gort. The two had come to deliver an important message of peace to the entire planet.

Glossary

allegations claims that someone has done something wrong

altitude the height of an object or point in relation to sea level or ground level

astonishment a feeling of great surprise or wonder

binary something made up of two parts or things

broadcasts messages or programs sent out on radio or television

canyon a deep valley with steep sides, often carved by a river

comet a ball of dust and ice in space that is visible from Earth

commercial a product or service for the public sold in order to make money

concentric repeated shapes that start at a center point and get bigger and bigger

contaminated made dirty by adding something harmful

coverup an attempt to hide the truth about something

credible believable or trustworthy

crescent a curved shape that is wide in the center and pointed at the ends like a crescent moon

detached separated or not connected to anything

devastation great destruction or damage

disembodied separated from or lacking a physical body

disfigured changed or ruined by injury or some other cause

documented recorded in writing or other form for future reference

echelon a flight formation in which aircraft fly at a certain elevation above or below and a certain distance behind and to the right or left of the craft ahead

encounter a meeting, especially one that is unexpected

evidence information or objects that help prove something is true or not

extraterrestrial relating to something from outside Earth or its atmosphere

fragmented broken into small parts

glistening shining with a sparkling light

hoax a trick or deception meant to fool people

humanoid having an appearance resembling that of a human

hydrogen a light, colorless gas that is the most abundant element in the universe

hypnosis a relaxed, trance state where people can recall lost memories

incapacitate to prevent from functioning in a normal way

interpretations ways of explaining or understanding things

intervals spaces of time or distance between things

manipulating controlling or influencing something or someone

mysterious difficult to understand or explain; full of secrets

negatives photographic images on transparent material used for printing positive images

penetrating having the power of entering; appearing to have special insight

phenomena occurrences that one can seen or feel

prompted caused or brought about an action or feeling

reconstruct to conceptually re-create the pieces of an event

remote secluded or far removed from other things

ridicule making fun of someone or something in a mean way

skeptical an attitude of doubt or disbelief about something

therapeutic related to healing or making someone feel better

transparent clear and see-through

trauma a serious injury or distressing experience

ulcer a sore on the skin or inside the body that does not heal easily

weather balloon a balloon carrying special equipment that is sent into the atmosphere to provide information about the weather

Read More

Grace, N. B. *UFO Mysteries (Reading Rocks!).* Mankato, MN: The Child's World, 2022.

Kim, Carol. *Area 51 Alien and UFO Mysteries (History's Mysteries).* North Mankato, MN: Capstone Press, 2022.

Marcovitz, Hal. *UFOs and Alien Encounters: Are They Real?* San Diego, CA: ReferencePoint Press, Inc., 2022.

Spilsbury, Louise. *Alien Visitations (History Raiders).* New York: Crabtree Publishing, 2022.

Learn More Online

1. Go to **FactSurfer.com** or scan the QR code below.
2. Enter "**Alien Visits**" into the search box.
3. Click on the cover of this book to see a list of websites.

Index